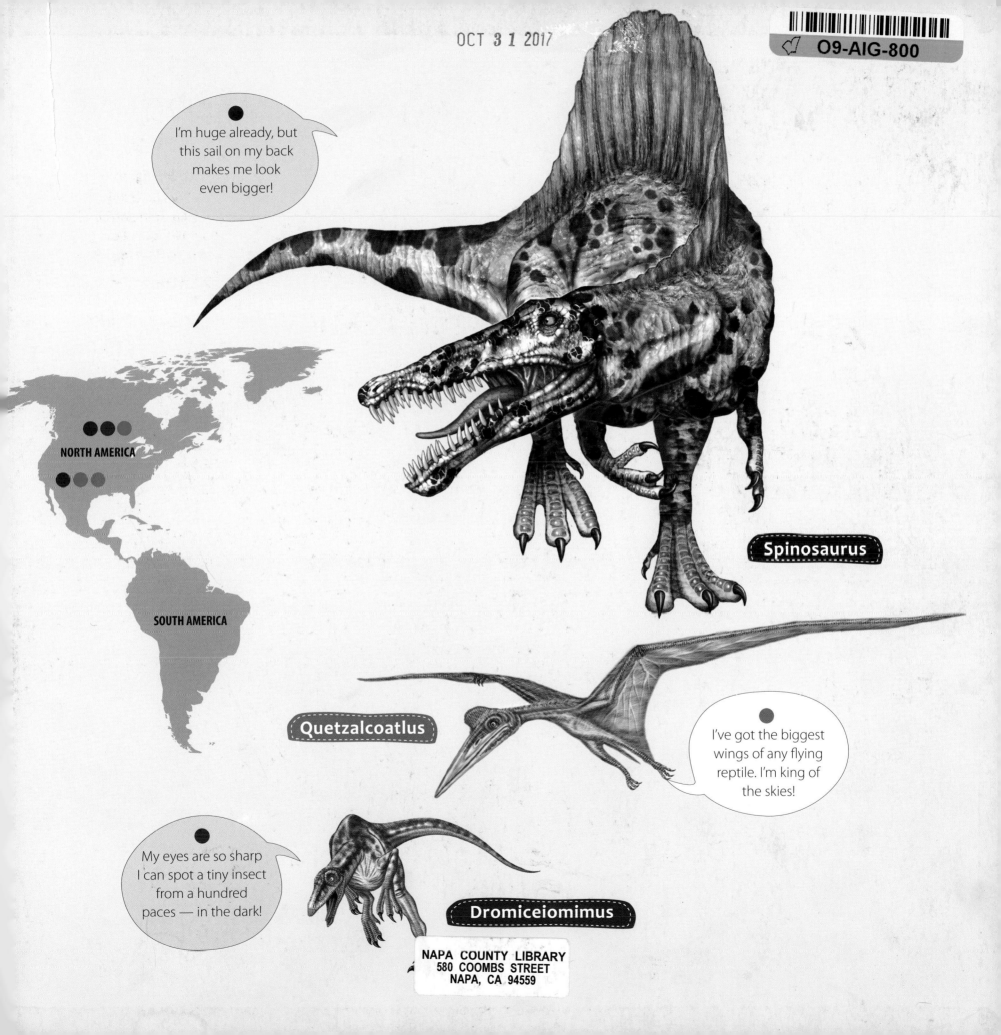

big & SMALL

Original Korean text and illustrations by Dreaming Tortoise
Korean edition © Aram Publishing

This English edition published by big & SMALL in 2017
by arrangement with Aram Publishing
English text edited by Scott Forbes
English edition © big & SMALL 2017

Distributed in the United States and Canada by
Lerner Publishing Group, Inc.
241 First Avenue North
Minneapolis, MN 55401 U.S.A.
www.lernerbooks.com

Photo credits:
Page 28, top:© Domser
Page 29, top: © Kabacchi; center: © Piotrus

To learn more about dinosaur fossils, see page 28.
For information on the main groups of dinosaurs,
see the Dinosaur Family Tree on page 30.

Armored
Ankylosaurus

Ankylosaurus

big & SMALL

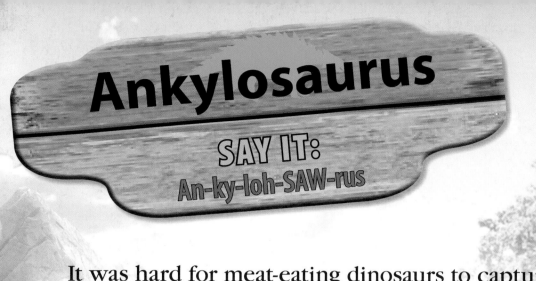

Ankylosaurus

It was hard for meat-eating dinosaurs to capture an Ankylosaurus. That's because this big plant-eater's back was covered in hard, bony plates and spikes — a bit like a suit of armor! Also, Ankylosaurus had a dangerous weapon: a huge tail club like a sledgehammer. One thump with that could break the bones or teeth of even the biggest meat-eater!

An Albertosaurus tried to attack an Ankylosaurus as it was eating. The Ankylosaurus swung its tail and whacked the huge meat-eater on its hip. Hurt, the Albertosaurus crept away, to look for easier prey!

ALBERTOSAURUS

GROUP: Theropods
DIET: Meat
WHEN IT LIVED: Late Cretaceous
WHERE IT LIVED: North America (USA, Canada)
LENGTH: 30 feet (9 meters)
HEIGHT: 13 feet (4 meters)
WEIGHT: 1.6 tons (1.5 tonnes)

7

If Ankylosaurus couldn't keep an attacker away by swinging its tail, it would sometimes just lie down on the ground. This protected its soft underparts and meant the attacker had to try to rip or bite through its hard armor.

Though the armor on Ankylosaurus' back was heavy, it was made up of lots of small, bony plates, which were connected to each other by stretchy muscles. This allowed Ankylosaurus to move quite freely.

HEIGHT: 11.5 feet (3.5 meters)

LENGTH: 26–33 feet (8–10 meters)

WEIGHT: 6.6–8.8 tons (6–8 tonnes)

WHEN IT LIVED: TRIASSIC JURASSIC CRETACEOUS

GROUP: Ankylosaurs

DIET: Plants

WHERE IT LIVED:
North America (USA, Canada)
Asia (South Korea)

Psittacosaurus

In the middle of the forest, a group of Psittacosaurus were munching on their favorite plants. One of them suddenly raised the alarm. It had spotted a group of fierce Dilongs approaching.

10

Psittacosaurus means "parrot lizard." The little dinosaur was given this name because its mouth was like the beak of a parrot.

Although Psittacosaurus did not have any teeth, its beak was sharp and strong enough to cut through tough stems and leaves.

DILONG

GROUP: Theropods
DIET: Meat
WHEN IT LIVED: Early Cretaceous
WHERE IT LIVED: Asia (China)
LENGTH: 6.6 feet (2 meters)
HEIGHT: 2.6 feet (0.8 meters)
WEIGHT: 22 pounds
(10 kilograms)

Psittacosaurus moved around on two legs. Its arms were not long enough to reach the ground or strong enough to support its weight.

The Psittacosaurus ran away as fast as they could, zigzagging through the trees to try to lose their pursuers. They found a clump of bushes and decided to take cover there.

But as soon as they entered the bushes, they got a terrific fright. Hidden in there were several Microraptors — small but fierce meat-eating, bird-like dinosaurs.

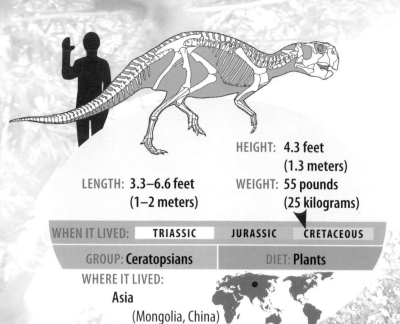

HEIGHT:	4.3 feet
	(1.3 meters)
LENGTH: 3.3–6.6 feet	WEIGHT: 55 pounds
(1–2 meters)	(25 kilograms)

| WHEN IT LIVED: | TRIASSIC | JURASSIC | CRETACEOUS |

| GROUP: Ceratopsians | DIET: Plants |

WHERE IT LIVED:
Asia
(Mongolia, China)

Psittacosaurus is the ancestor of the much larger horned dinosaurs, or ceratopsians, that appeared later in the age of the dinosaurs, such as Triceratops.

Once again, the Psittacosaurus had to do what they always did in the face of danger — turn and run!

MICRORAPTOR

GROUP: Theropods
DIET: Meat
WHEN IT LIVED: Early Cretaceous
WHERE IT LIVED: Asia (China, Korea)
LENGTH: 1.3–2.6 feet (40–80 centimeters)
HEIGHT: 1.3 feet (40 centimeters)
WEIGHT: 4.4–8.8 pounds
(2–4 kilograms)

13

Hypacrosaurus

SAY IT:
Hy-pak-roh-SAW-rus

A female Hypacrosaurus was keeping watch over its young. They were still very small and it was one of their first outings, so the mother was alert for danger.

Sure enough, she saw a pair of Dromaeosaurus approaching. They were too small to attack her but might snatch up one of her young. She signaled for the babies to run back to the main Hypacrosaurus herd.

DROMAEOSAURUS

GROUP: Theropods
DIET: Meat
WHEN IT LIVED: Late Cretaceous
WHERE IT LIVED: North America
(USA, Canada)
LENGTH: 6 feet (1.8 meters)
HEIGHT: 4.3 feet (1.3 meters)
WEIGHT: 33–77 pounds
(15–35 kilograms)

Hypacrosaurus means "near the highest lizard." The dinosaur was given this name because it was very large — almost as big as a Tyrannosaurus. It was, however, a gentle plant-eater.

HEIGHT: 10 feet (3 meters)

LENGTH: 23–30 feet (7–9 meters)

WEIGHT: 3.3–4.4 tons (3–4 tonnes)

WHEN IT LIVED: TRIASSIC | JURASSIC | CRETACEOUS

GROUP: Ornithopods

DIET: Plants

WHERE IT LIVED: North America (USA, Canada)

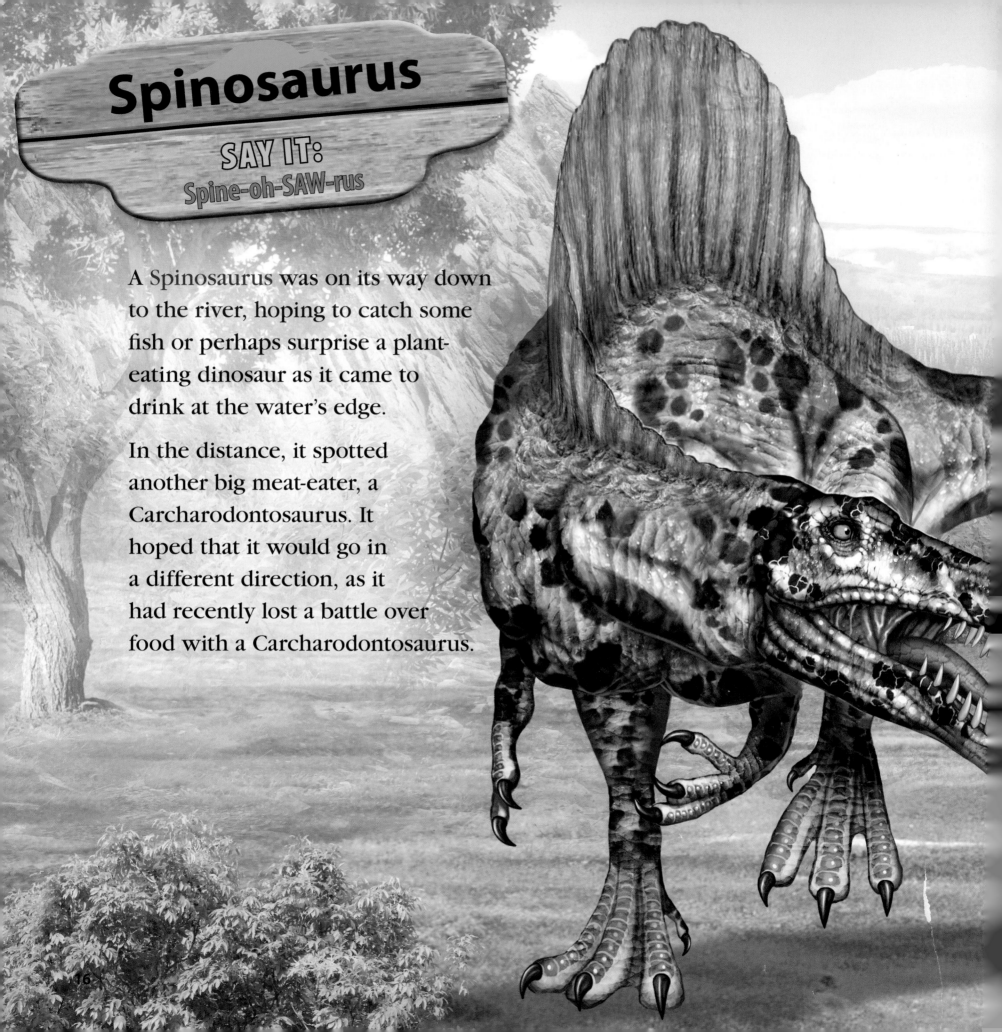

Spinosaurus

SAY IT:
Spine-oh-SAW-rus

A Spinosaurus was on its way down to the river, hoping to catch some fish or perhaps surprise a plant-eating dinosaur as it came to drink at the water's edge.

In the distance, it spotted another big meat-eater, a Carcharodontosaurus. It hoped that it would go in a different direction, as it had recently lost a battle over food with a Carcharodontosaurus.

Spinosaurus was an enormous meat-eating dinosaur that lived in Africa. Its only rival in size was Carcharodontosaurus. Usually these two dinosaurs kept out of each other's way, but occasionally they clashed.

LENGTH: 33–60 feet (10–18 meters)

HEIGHT: 18 feet (5.5 meters)

WEIGHT: 8.8 tons (8 tonnes)

WHEN IT LIVED: TRIASSIC | JURASSIC | CRETACEOUS

GROUP: Theropods

DIET: Meat

WHERE IT LIVED: Africa (Egypt, Morocco)

The Spinosaurus lost sight of the Carcharodontosaurus and continued on its way to the river. But no sooner had it snatched up a fish than it heard a noise behind it. It turned to face the massive Carcharodontosaurus, which was ready to attack. Who would win the battle of the giants?

CARCHARODONTOSAURUS

GROUP: Theropods
DIET: Meat
WHEN IT LIVED: Early to Late Cretaceous
WHERE IT LIVED: Africa (Algeria,
Niger, Morocco)
LENGTH: 40–46 feet (12–14 meters)
HEIGHT: 20 feet (6 meters)
WEIGHT: 6.6–8.3 tons
(6–7.5 tonnes)

Spinosaurus means "spine lizard." This giant dinosaur had vertical spines along its back that held up a sheath, or sail, of skin. This made Spinosaurus look even bigger.

Quetzalcoatlus

SAY IT:
Ket-sull-ko-AT-lus

The Quetzalcoatlus ran toward the edge of the cliff, leaped into the air, then soared high into the sky on its enormous wings. It joined a group of other Quetzalcoatlus as they swooped down to a deep lake flanked by waterfalls. One by one they dived toward the water to try to catch fish.

Quetzalcoatlus was named after a famous god of the Aztec people of Mexico, a great feathered serpent called Quetzalcoatl.

One of the Quetzalcoatlus spotted something interesting. A Lambeosaurus had been attacked and killed by a meat-eater and left lying on the ground. The Quetzalcoatlus all flew down and landed beside it. Then they started tearing at its flesh.

LAMBEOSAURUS

GROUP: Ornithopods
DIET: Plants
WHEN IT LIVED: Late Cretaceous
WHERE IT LIVED: North America
(USA, Canada, Mexico)
LENGTH: 26 feet (8 meters)
HEIGHT: 8 feet (2.5 meters)
WEIGHT: 3.3–9.4 tons
(3–8.5 tonnes)

Quetzalcoatlus was the biggest flying reptile, or pterosaur, of all. With a wingspan of up to 40 feet (12 meters), it was about the size of a small plane. When it stood upright on the ground it was up to 10 feet (3 meters) tall. However, its bones were hollow, which made it quite light and helped it get off the ground with ease.

HEIGHT: 10 feet (3 meters)

WINGSPAN: 36–40 feet (11–12 meters)

WEIGHT: 200 pounds (90 kilograms)

WHEN IT LIVED: TRIASSIC   JURASSIC   CRETACEOUS

GROUP: Pterosaurs

DIET: Meat

WHERE IT LIVED: North America (USA)

Dromiceiomimus

SAY IT:
Dro-mee-see-oh-MY-mus

The Dromiceiomimus were scurrying around in the forest, looking on the ground and under bushes and rocks for little creatures. Suddenly, one of them spotted a lizard and they all charged toward it. But the lizard sped into a crack in a rock and vanished from sight.

Dromiceiomimus was small and had a weak jaw, so it couldn't eat larger creatures. Instead it spent all its time hunting for small reptiles and insects. Its eyes were big and sharp and it could spot tiny creatures from a distance, even in the dark.

Dromiceiomimus means "emu mimic." Scientists chose this name for the dinosaur because it had long legs and a long neck, like those of an emu.

The Dromiceiomimus next came across a nest full of eggs. What luck! They started gathering up the eggs, but then they heard a loud roaring. A Gorgosaurus was charging toward them! The terrified Dromiceiomimus started running as fast as they could.

LENGTH: **12 feet**
(3.6 meters)

HEIGHT: **3.3 feet**
(1 meter)

WEIGHT: **200 pounds**
(90 kilograms)

WHEN IT LIVED: | **TRIASSIC** | **JURASSIC** | **CRETACEOUS**

GROUP: **Theropods**

DIET: **Meat**

WHERE IT LIVED:
North America
(Canada)

Dromiceiomimus was light, with strong back legs and it could run extremely fast. Few dinosaurs could match it for speed.

Dromiceiomimus was also fairly intelligent, so it was good at finding escape routes!

GORGOSAURUS

GROUP: Theropods
DIET: Meat
WHEN IT LIVED: Late Cretaceous
WHERE IT LIVED: North America
(USA, Canada)
LENGTH: 26 feet (8 meters)
HEIGHT: 8 feet (2.5 meters)
WEIGHT: 2.8 tons
(2.5 tonnes)

Dinosaur Fossils

Fossils are the remains of dinosaurs. They can be hard parts of dinosaurs, such as bones and teeth, that have slowly turned to stone. Or they may be impressions of bones, teeth, or skin preserved in rocks.

▲ Model of an Ankylosaurus tailbone

Ankylosaurus

The first Ankylosaurus' fossil was discovered at Hell Creek in Montana, USA, in 1906. Many others have been found since, including some from the very end of the age of the dinosaurs. That means Ankylosaurus was probably among the last group of dinosaurs to live on Earth.

Psittacosaurus

Psittacosaurus was discovered in 1922, when an expedition from the American Museum of Natural History traveled to the Gobi Desert in Mongolia. It found a number of new dinosaurs, including Psittacosaurus, which was named the following year by American dinosaur expert Henry Fairfield Osborn. Many more Psittacosaurus fossils have since been found in Mongolia and northern China.

▲ Model of Psittacosaurus adult and juvenile skeletons

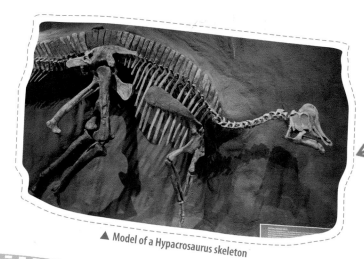

▲ Model of a Hypacrosaurus skeleton

Hypacrosaurus

The first Hypacrosaurus fossils to be found, at Red Deer River in Alberta, Canada in 1910, included a set of about 20 fossilized eggs in a nest, as well as fossils of many baby and juvenile Hypacrosaurus. By studying a number of fossils, scientists were able to work out that Hypacrosaurus' crest grew larger as it got older.

Spinosaurus

▲ Spinosaurus head and neck bones

Spinosaurus was first discovered in Egypt, Africa, in 1912 by a German fossil hunter called Ralph Markgraf. He took the fossils back to a museum in Munich, where they were put on display in a grand hall. Unfortunately the display, and much of the museum, was completely destroyed by bombing during World War II. Scientists have had to use drawings of this specimen and a few other small fossils found since then to try to work out the exact shape of Spinosaurus.

Quetzalcoatlus

The first Quetzalcoatlus fossil was found in Texas, USA, in 1971. Scientists were amazed not only by this flying reptile's enormous wingspan, but also by its very long neck — which was longer than that of a giraffe! This neck was strong enough to support the reptile's huge head and allowed it to stretch down and scoop up prey as it swooped over water.

▲ Model of a Quetzalcoatlus skeleton

Dromiceiomimus

▲ Model of a Dromiceiomimus fossil

When the first Dromiceiomimus fossil was found, it was thought to be another ostrich-like dinosaur called Struthiomimus. However, a Canadian dinosaur expert, Dale Russell, gradually recognized clear differences between the new discovery and existing Struthiomimus fossils, and decided it was a separate type. In 1972, the new dinosaur was named Dromiceiomimus.

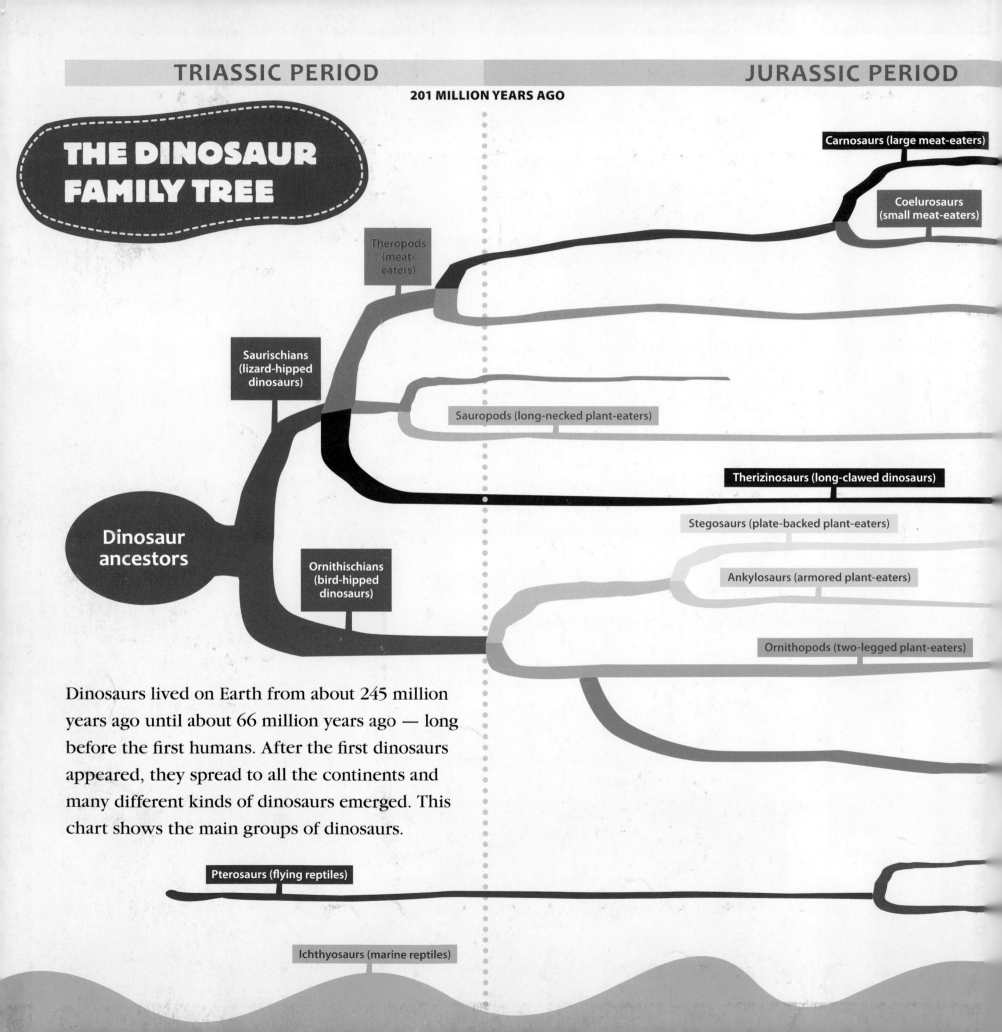

201 MILLION YEARS AGO

THE DINOSAUR FAMILY TREE

Carnosaurs (large meat-eaters)

Coelurosaurs (small meat-eaters)

Theropods (meat-eaters)

Saurischians (lizard-hipped dinosaurs)

Sauropods (long-necked plant-eaters)

Therizinosaurs (long-clawed dinosaurs)

Stegosaurs (plate-backed plant-eaters)

Dinosaur ancestors

Ornithischians (bird-hipped dinosaurs)

Ankylosaurs (armored plant-eaters)

Ornithopods (two-legged plant-eaters)

Dinosaurs lived on Earth from about 245 million years ago until about 66 million years ago — long before the first humans. After the first dinosaurs appeared, they spread to all the continents and many different kinds of dinosaurs emerged. This chart shows the main groups of dinosaurs.

Pterosaurs (flying reptiles)

Ichthyosaurs (marine reptiles)